Controversial Paths: Legal Aspects and Debates in the Invasion and Occupation of Iraq

Copyright Page

TITLE: Controversial Paths: Legal Aspects and Debates in the Invasion and Occupation of Iraq

1ST Edition

Copyright @ 2023

ISBN: 9798223121794

Table of Contents

Controversial Paths: Legal Aspects and Debates in the Invasion and Occupation of Iraq

By Roberto Miguel Rodriguez

Chapter 1: Operation Iraqi Freedom: The U.S.-led Invasion of Iraq and the Removal of Saddam Hussein

Background and Justification for the Invasion

The invasion and occupation of Iraq, known as Operation Iraqi Freedom, was a highly controversial event that shaped the course of international relations in the 21st century. This subchapter will delve into the background and justification for this military intervention, shedding light on the various factors that led to the decision to invade Iraq.

At the heart of the rationale for the invasion was the belief that Saddam Hussein, the dictator of Iraq at the time, possessed weapons of mass destruction (WMDs) and posed a significant threat to global security. The intelligence community, both in the United States and abroad, had reported the existence of these WMDs, although subsequent investigations failed to substantiate these claims. This subchapter will explore the role of intelligence in shaping the decision-making process and the subsequent hunt for these elusive weapons.

Moreover, the invasion was also justified on humanitarian grounds. The regime of Saddam Hussein was notorious for its brutal repression of its own people, and the invasion aimed to liberate the Iraqi population from his tyrannical rule. However, the subsequent civilian casualties and the challenges faced in providing humanitarian aid will also be discussed, highlighting the complexities and unintended consequences of such military interventions.

The political implications and aftermath of the U.S.-led invasion of Iraq were far-reaching. The removal of Saddam Hussein opened up a power vacuum, leading to sectarian tensions and instability that continue to plague the region to this day. This subchapter will analyze the political landscape post-invasion, examining the challenges faced by the occupying forces and the subsequent attempts at reconstruction.

The media coverage and propaganda surrounding Operation Iraqi Freedom played a crucial role in shaping public opinion. The subchapter will explore the role of the media in influencing public perception and the controversies surrounding the portrayal of the invasion in the press.

Furthermore, international relations and the role of coalition forces in the invasion will be examined. The subchapter will delve into the dynamics between the United States and its allies, as well as the reactions and criticisms from the international community.

Lastly, the subchapter will touch upon the economic impact and reconstruction efforts post-Saddam Hussein, the psychological and emotional toll on soldiers and veterans, the legal aspects and controversies surrounding the invasion and occupation, and public opinion and protests against Operation Iraqi Freedom.

By exploring these various dimensions, this subchapter aims to provide historians and readers with a comprehensive understanding of the background and justification for the controversial invasion and occupation of Iraq.

Coalition Forces and their Objectives

The invasion and occupation of Iraq by coalition forces, led by the United States, during Operation Iraqi Freedom were driven by a range of objectives that encompassed both military and political goals. This subchapter aims to provide a comprehensive understanding of the coalition forces' objectives and their implications in the context of the controversial invasion and occupation of Iraq.

From a military standpoint, the primary objective of the coalition forces was to topple Saddam Hussein's regime and remove him from power. Saddam Hussein's history of aggression, human rights abuses, and alleged possession of weapons of mass destruction posed a significant threat not only to regional stability but also to international security. The coalition forces aimed to neutralize these threats and establish a more democratic and stable Iraq.

In addition to the military objective, the coalition forces sought to implement a comprehensive political strategy. This involved supporting the establishment of a democratic government that would be representative of the diverse Iraqi population. The coalition aimed to empower the Iraqi people, promote human rights, and foster a spirit of inclusivity and reconciliation among different ethnic and religious groups.

Furthermore, the humanitarian aspect of the coalition forces' objectives cannot be understated. The invasion and subsequent conflict had a profound impact on the civilian population, resulting in significant casualties and displacement. The coalition forces aimed to provide humanitarian aid, protect civilian lives, and assist in the reconstruction efforts post-Saddam Hussein. However, the reality on the ground proved to be more complex, with civilian casualties and human rights abuses raising questions about the effectiveness of these efforts.

The subchapter will delve into the role of coalition forces in the invasion and occupation of Iraq, exploring the military strategy and tactics employed during Operation Iraqi Freedom. It will also analyze the political implications and aftermath of the invasion, including the establishment of a new government, nation-building efforts, and the challenges faced in rebuilding Iraq's infrastructure and institutions.

Moreover, the subchapter will examine the role of intelligence and the hunt for weapons of mass destruction in Iraq, a key justification for the invasion that ultimately proved to be unfounded. It will also explore the economic impact of the invasion and the subsequent reconstruction efforts, as well as the psychological and emotional toll on soldiers and veterans of Operation Iraqi Freedom.

By critically analyzing these facets, this subchapter aims to provide historians and niche audiences a comprehensive understanding of the coalition forces' objectives and the controversies surrounding the invasion and occupation of Iraq. It will shed light on the complexities and multifaceted nature of Operation Iraqi Freedom, inviting readers to engage in a nuanced exploration of this pivotal chapter in contemporary history.

Initial Military Operations and the Fall of Saddam Hussein

The subchapter titled "Initial Military Operations and the Fall of Saddam Hussein" explores the crucial moments and events that marked the beginning of the U.S.-led invasion of Iraq and the subsequent removal of Saddam Hussein from power. This chapter aims to provide historians with a comprehensive analysis of the military strategy and tactics employed during Operation Iraqi Freedom, the political implications and aftermath of the invasion, and the various controversies and debates surrounding this controversial period in history.

The chapter delves into the intricacies of the initial military operations, highlighting the meticulous planning and execution of the invasion by the coalition forces. It examines the key battles and military campaigns that led to the eventual capture and overthrow of Saddam Hussein, examining both the successes and challenges faced by the invading forces. Additionally, it sheds light on the role of intelligence and the hunt for weapons of mass destruction in Iraq, which played a significant part in justifying the invasion.

Furthermore, this subchapter addresses the political implications and aftermath of the U.S.-led invasion of Iraq. It analyzes the shift in power dynamics, the establishment of a transitional government, and the subsequent challenges faced in stabilizing the country. It also explores the economic impact and reconstruction efforts post-Saddam Hussein, providing insights into the complexities of rebuilding a nation torn apart by conflict.

The chapter also acknowledges the humanitarian efforts and civilian casualties during the invasion. It emphasizes the importance of understanding the human cost of war and the challenges faced by both the military and non-combatant populations. Moreover, it critically examines the media coverage and propaganda surrounding Operation Iraqi Freedom, shedding light on the role of the media in shaping public perception and influencing global opinion.

Lastly, this subchapter considers the international relations and the role of coalition forces in the invasion. It explores the dynamics between the United States and its allies, highlighting the complexities of operating within a multinational force. It also addresses the psychological and emotional toll on soldiers and veterans of Operation Iraqi Freedom, providing a nuanced understanding of the long-lasting impact of war on those who served.

By examining the legal aspects and controversies surrounding the invasion and occupation of Iraq, this chapter aims to provide historians with a comprehensive understanding of the multifaceted nature of Operation Iraqi Freedom. Taking into account the various niches and interests of the audience, it offers a balanced perspective on this significant period in history, addressing public opinion and protests against the invasion, as well as the broader implications for international law and humanitarian norms.

Resistance and Insurgency Movements

Throughout history, resistance and insurgency movements have played a significant role in shaping the outcomes of conflicts and challenging occupying forces. In the context of the U.S.-led invasion of Iraq and the subsequent occupation, the emergence of resistance and insurgency movements had a profound impact on the course of events and the long-term consequences of Operation Iraqi Freedom.

The resistance movement in Iraq can be traced back to the early days of the invasion when various factions, motivated by different causes, began to organize against the occupying forces. This subchapter will delve into the origins, strategies, and motivations of these resistance movements, shedding light on the diverse array of actors involved, including former members of Saddam Hussein's regime, Islamist militants, and nationalist groups.

One of the key factors that fueled the growth of resistance and insurgency movements was the failure of the U.S.-led coalition to adequately plan for the post-invasion phase. This lack of planning left a power vacuum in Iraq, which allowed various groups to exploit the situation and rally support against the occupying forces. Moreover, the mishandling of de-Baathification policies and the disbanding of the Iraqi army further exacerbated the grievances and grievances within the Iraqi population, providing fertile ground for insurgency movements to gain traction.

This subchapter will explore the military strategies and tactics employed by the resistance movements, including guerrilla warfare, suicide bombings, and hit-and-run attacks. It will also analyze the political implications and aftermath of these movements, such as their impact on the overall security situation in Iraq, the effectiveness of counterinsurgency efforts, and the challenges faced by coalition forces in combating an elusive and decentralized enemy.

Furthermore, this subchapter will examine the humanitarian efforts and civilian casualties during the invasion and occupation, shedding light on the ethical dilemmas faced by both the occupying forces and the resistance movements. It will also delve into the media coverage and propaganda surrounding Operation Iraqi Freedom, exploring the role of the media in shaping public opinion and the narratives surrounding the conflict.

By examining the resistance and insurgency movements in Iraq, this subchapter aims to provide historians with a comprehensive understanding of the complexities and challenges faced during the U.S.-led invasion and occupation. It will shed light on the multifaceted nature of these movements, their impact on the military, political, and humanitarian aspects of the conflict, and their long-term consequences for the region and the world. Through this analysis, historians can gain valuable insights into the dynamics of insurgency and counterinsurgency operations, informing future military strategies and policies in similar contexts.

Chapter 2: Military Strategy and Tactics during Operation Iraqi Freedom

Planning and Execution of the Invasion

The planning and execution of the invasion of Iraq, known as Operation Iraqi Freedom, was a complex and controversial process that had far-reaching consequences. This subchapter delves into the intricacies and debates surrounding this crucial phase, providing a comprehensive understanding for historians studying this pivotal period.

The invasion was the result of years of planning and strategizing by the U.S.-led coalition forces. Military experts meticulously studied the terrain, intelligence reports, and the capabilities of Saddam Hussein's regime. This subchapter examines the military strategy and tactics employed during Operation Iraqi Freedom, shedding light on the decisions made by commanders on the ground and the effectiveness of their approaches.

However, the invasion was not solely a military operation. It had significant political implications and an enduring aftermath. This subchapter explores the political landscape leading up to the invasion, including the debates within the United States and on the international stage. It also delves into the consequences of the invasion, such as the establishment of a new government and the challenges faced during the transition period.

The humanitarian efforts and civilian casualties during the invasion are also examined in this subchapter. It analyzes the impact of the invasion on Iraqi civilians, the challenges faced by humanitarian organizations, and the controversies surrounding the number of civilian casualties. Additionally, it delves into the media coverage and propaganda surrounding Operation Iraqi Freedom, highlighting the role of media in shaping public opinion and influencing the narrative of the invasion.

Furthermore, this subchapter explores the role of coalition forces and international relations during the invasion. It examines the contributions of various countries to the coalition, the challenges faced by multinational forces, and the diplomatic implications of the invasion on the global stage.

The hunt for weapons of mass destruction (WMDs) in Iraq was a central aspect of the invasion. This subchapter delves into the role of intelligence in shaping the decision to invade and the subsequent search for WMDs. It scrutinizes the controversy surrounding the intelligence assessments and the consequences of the failure to find substantial evidence of WMDs.

The economic impact and reconstruction efforts post-Saddam Hussein are also discussed in this subchapter. It delves into the challenges faced in rebuilding Iraq's infrastructure, the allocation of funds, and the effectiveness of reconstruction efforts.

Moreover, the psychological and emotional toll on soldiers and veterans of Operation Iraqi Freedom is addressed. It explores the experiences of soldiers on the ground, examining the impact of combat and the challenges faced by veterans upon their return home.

Lastly, this subchapter delves into the legal aspects and controversies surrounding the invasion and occupation of Iraq. It analyzes the justifications provided by the coalition forces, the debates surrounding the legality of the invasion, and the implications for international law.

Overall, this subchapter provides a comprehensive analysis of the planning and execution of the invasion of Iraq, addressing the various aspects and controversies that surround Operation Iraqi Freedom. It is an essential resource for historians and anyone interested in understanding this pivotal period in history.

Air Campaign and Bombing Operations

The air campaign and bombing operations during the U.S.-led invasion of Iraq, known as Operation Iraqi Freedom, played a crucial role in the overall military strategy and tactics employed. This subchapter delves into the various aspects of these operations, highlighting their significance, controversies, and consequences.

From the outset of the invasion, the U.S. and its coalition forces heavily relied on aerial bombardment to weaken Saddam Hussein's regime and his military capabilities. The objective was to degrade Iraq's air defenses, disrupt command and control structures, and destroy key infrastructure, communication networks, and military installations. The air campaign targeted not only strategic military sites but also Saddam Hussein's palaces and residences, aiming to undermine his hold on power.

The bombing operations involved a combination of precision airstrikes, conducted by fighter jets and unmanned drones, and the use of cruise missiles. The goal was to minimize civilian casualties while maximizing the destruction of enemy targets. However, despite the efforts to minimize collateral damage, reports of civilian casualties and damage to non-military targets emerged, sparking debates about the proportionality and legality of the airstrikes.

The media coverage and propaganda surrounding Operation Iraqi Freedom further complicated the perception of the air campaign and bombing operations. The U.S. government employed sophisticated media strategies to shape public opinion and garner support for the invasion. However, these efforts were met with skepticism from some quarters, leading to allegations of manipulation and misinformation.

Moreover, the psychological and emotional toll on soldiers and veterans involved in these operations cannot be overlooked. The air campaign exposed them to high-stress situations, including participating in airstrikes that resulted in civilian casualties. The long-term impact on their mental health and well-being remains a subject of ongoing research and concern.

Additionally, the hunt for weapons of mass destruction (WMDs) in Iraq was a driving force behind the invasion. The air campaign and bombing operations aimed to disable any suspected WMD sites. However, the failure to find substantial evidence of WMDs raised questions about the intelligence used to justify the invasion and the legality of the entire operation.

In conclusion, the air campaign and bombing operations during the U.S.-led invasion of Iraq were integral to the overall military strategy. However, they were not without controversy and consequences. The debates surrounding civilian casualties, media coverage, the hunt for WMDs, and the psychological toll on soldiers highlight the complex nature of these operations. Understanding and analyzing these aspects are crucial for historians studying Operation Iraqi Freedom and its implications on various niches, including military strategy, political implications, international relations, and the legal controversies surrounding the invasion and occupation of Iraq.

Ground Assault and Urban Warfare

The subchapter titled "Ground Assault and Urban Warfare" delves into the military strategy and tactics employed during the U.S.-led invasion of Iraq, specifically focusing on the challenges and controversies surrounding ground assaults and urban warfare. This chapter provides a comprehensive analysis of the intricacies involved in conducting military operations in an urban environment and the legal implications arising from these actions.

The invasion of Iraq, known as Operation Iraqi Freedom, presented unique challenges to the coalition forces. As they advanced through the country, they encountered densely populated cities, such as Baghdad, where street-to-street fighting became the norm. The chapter discusses the tactics utilized by the coalition forces to navigate these treacherous urban landscapes, including house-to-house searches, the use of armored vehicles, and the coordination of air support.

Furthermore, the chapter sheds light on the political implications and aftermath of ground assaults and urban warfare. It explores the impact of these operations on civilian populations, humanitarian efforts, and the significant number of civilian casualties that occurred during the invasion. The media coverage and propaganda surrounding Operation Iraqi Freedom are also examined, highlighting the role of the media in shaping public perception and the controversies arising from differing narratives.

Additionally, the subchapter addresses the international relations aspect of the invasion, emphasizing the role of coalition forces and their contributions to the military campaign. It analyzes the intelligence gathering process and the hunt for weapons of mass destruction in Iraq, exploring the controversies and legal aspects surrounding the decision to invade.

Moreover, the economic impact and reconstruction efforts post-Saddam Hussein are discussed, providing historians with insights into the challenges faced by the occupying forces in rebuilding the nation. The psychological and emotional toll on soldiers and veterans of Operation Iraqi Freedom are also examined, shedding light on the long-term effects of their experiences in urban warfare.

By delving into the legal aspects and controversies surrounding the invasion and occupation of Iraq, this subchapter provides historians with a comprehensive understanding of the complex dynamics that unfolded during the U.S.-led invasion. It addresses the public opinion and protests against Operation Iraqi Freedom, highlighting the debates and controversies that continue to shape our understanding of this significant historical event.

Overall, this subchapter offers historians a nuanced analysis of ground assaults and urban warfare during the invasion of Iraq, examining the military tactics employed, the legal implications, and the wider social, political, and economic consequences of these actions.

Challenges and Lessons Learned in Military Operations

Introduction:

The subchapter titled "Challenges and Lessons Learned in Military Operations" explores the various obstacles faced during the U.S.-led invasion of Iraq, known as Operation Iraqi Freedom. This section aims to provide historians and niche audiences with an in-depth understanding of the military strategy, political implications, humanitarian efforts, media coverage, international relations, intelligence, economic impact, psychological toll, legal aspects, and public opinion surrounding the invasion and occupation of Iraq.

1. Military Strategy and Tactics:

The invasion of Iraq presented numerous challenges in terms of military strategy and tactics. Historians will delve into the complexities of coordinating a large-scale operation, including the use of airpower, ground troops, and special operations forces. The subchapter will also explore the effectiveness of these strategies in achieving the mission's objectives.

2. Political Implications and Aftermath:

Operation Iraqi Freedom had significant political implications, both within Iraq and the international community. The chapter will examine the consequences of removing Saddam Hussein, the establishment of a new government, and the subsequent power struggles. It will also explore the impact of the invasion on regional stability and the broader Middle East.

3. Humanitarian Efforts and Civilian Casualties:

The invasion of Iraq had a profound impact on civilians, leading to a humanitarian crisis that historians will analyze. This section will discuss the challenges faced by military forces in providing aid and protection to Iraqi civilians. It will also shed light on the civilian casualties resulting from the invasion and the subsequent efforts to mitigate harm.

4. Media Coverage and Propaganda:

The subchapter will explore the media coverage of Operation Iraqi Freedom, including the role of embedded journalists and the dissemination of propaganda. Historians will examine how the media's portrayal of the conflict shaped public opinion and influenced the perception of the war both domestically and internationally.

5. International Relations and Coalition Forces:

The role of coalition forces in the invasion and occupation of Iraq will be thoroughly examined. Historians will analyze the dynamics between the United States and its allies, as well as the challenges faced in coordinating multinational military operations. The subchapter will also explore the impact of the invasion on international relations in the post-9/11 era.

6. Intelligence and the Hunt for Weapons of Mass Destruction:

The subchapter will delve into the role of intelligence agencies in the lead-up to the invasion, focusing on the hunt for weapons of mass destruction (WMDs). Historians will assess the accuracy of intelligence reports and the subsequent controversies surrounding the absence of WMDs. They will also explore the implications of this intelligence failure on subsequent military operations.

7. Economic Impact and Reconstruction Efforts:

The economic impact of the invasion and the subsequent efforts to rebuild Iraq will be thoroughly examined. Historians will analyze the challenges faced in stabilizing the economy and reconstructing the country's infrastructure. They will also explore the role of international organizations and the allocation of resources during the reconstruction process.

8. Psychological and Emotional Toll on Soldiers and Veterans:

Operation Iraqi Freedom had a significant psychological and emotional toll on soldiers and veterans. This section will delve into the challenges faced by military personnel, including combat stress, post-traumatic stress disorder (PTSD), and the difficulties in reintegrating into civilian life. Historians will also explore the support systems in place for soldiers and the long-term impact on their wellbeing.

9. Legal Aspects and Controversies:

The subchapter will explore the legal aspects and controversies surrounding the invasion and occupation of Iraq. Historians will examine the justifications for the war, including debates on international law and the United Nations Security Council resolutions. They will also analyze the legal implications of detainee abuse and the establishment of military tribunals.

10. Public Opinion and Protests:

This section will explore the public opinion and protests against Operation Iraqi Freedom. Historians will analyze the anti-war movements, both domestically and internationally, and assess their impact on policy decisions. They will also examine the role of public opinion in shaping the narrative of the war and influencing subsequent military actions.

Conclusion:

"Challenges and Lessons Learned in Military Operations" provides historians and niche audiences with a comprehensive analysis of the complexities and controversies surrounding the invasion and occupation of Iraq. By examining the military strategy, political implications, humanitarian efforts, media coverage, international relations, intelligence, economic impact, psychological toll, legal aspects, and public opinion, this subchapter offers a nuanced understanding of Operation Iraqi Freedom and its lasting effects.

Chapter 3: Political Implications and Aftermath of the U.S.-led Invasion of Iraq

Establishment of a New Government

In the aftermath of the U.S.-led invasion of Iraq and the removal of Saddam Hussein, the establishment of a new government became a crucial task. This subchapter explores the challenges and controversies surrounding this process, shedding light on the legal aspects and debates that shaped the post-invasion era in Iraq.

One of the primary objectives of Operation Iraqi Freedom was to pave the way for a democratic government that would represent the will of the Iraqi people. However, the task of establishing a new government proved to be complex and multifaceted. The military strategy and tactics employed during the invasion played a pivotal role in dismantling the existing regime, but the subsequent political implications and aftermath posed significant challenges.

The removal of Saddam Hussein left a political power vacuum, leading to a struggle for authority among various factions and ethnic groups. This chapter delves into the intricacies of this power struggle and its impact on the establishment of a stable and inclusive government. It examines the role of coalition forces in managing this transition and the challenges they faced in navigating Iraq's complex sectarian dynamics.

Furthermore, this subchapter delves into the legal aspects and controversies surrounding the invasion and occupation of Iraq. It explores the international legal justifications for the intervention, including debates around the legitimacy of preemptive self-defense and the role of the United Nations. It also scrutinizes the hunt for weapons of mass destruction, the intelligence failures, and the implications of these controversies on the overall legitimacy of the invasion.

The establishment of a new government also had far-reaching economic and reconstruction implications. This chapter investigates the economic impact of Saddam Hussein's removal and the subsequent efforts to rebuild Iraq's infrastructure, institutions, and economy. It examines the challenges faced in this process and the controversies surrounding the awarding of contracts to foreign firms.

Finally, this subchapter addresses the psychological and emotional toll on soldiers and veterans of Operation Iraqi Freedom. It delves into the experiences of those who served on the ground, highlighting the long-lasting effects of the war on their mental health and overall well-being.

Overall, this subchapter provides historians with a comprehensive understanding of the establishment of a new government in post-invasion Iraq. It critically examines the legal, political, economic, and social dimensions of this process, shedding light on the controversies and challenges that shaped the post-Saddam era. By exploring these complexities, it enables historians to gain deeper insights into the broader context of Operation Iraqi Freedom and its aftermath.

Sectarian Conflicts and Rise of Insurgency

The subchapter "Sectarian Conflicts and Rise of Insurgency" delves into one of the most significant and consequential aspects of the invasion and occupation of Iraq. Addressing historians and those interested in Operation Iraqi Freedom, this subchapter explores the intricate dynamics that unfolded during this period, shedding light on the complex relationship between sectarian conflicts and the subsequent rise of insurgency.

The invasion of Iraq in 2003, led by the United States, aimed to remove Saddam Hussein from power and bring stability to the region. However, the power vacuum left in the wake of Hussein's removal ignited long-standing sectarian tensions that had been suppressed under his regime. Historically, Iraq had been plagued by sectarian divisions between the Sunni and Shiite populations, and these divisions resurfaced with a vengeance.

The subchapter delves into the factors that fueled sectarian conflicts, such as religious differences, power struggles, and the manipulation of sectarian sentiments by various actors. It examines how the dismantling of Iraq's Ba'athist regime, which had suppressed sectarian tensions, inadvertently paved the way for the rise of insurgency groups, particularly Sunni extremist organizations like Al-Qaeda in Iraq.

Moreover, the subchapter explores the impact of the sectarian conflicts and insurgency on the military strategy and tactics employed during Operation Iraqi Freedom. It analyzes how the U.S.-led coalition forces had to adapt their approach to counter the growing insurgency, including the implementation of counterinsurgency measures, such as targeted operations, intelligence-driven tactics, and the establishment of local security forces.

The ramifications of the sectarian conflicts and insurgency extended beyond military strategy and tactics. The subchapter also addresses the political implications and aftermath of the U.S.-led invasion, shedding light on the challenges faced by the newly formed Iraqi government in reconciling sectarian divisions and establishing a stable political system. It further examines the humanitarian efforts and civilian casualties during the invasion, underscoring the profound impact of sectarian tensions on the Iraqi population.

Additionally, the subchapter highlights the role of media coverage and propaganda surrounding Operation Iraqi Freedom, discussing how the portrayal of sectarian conflicts and insurgency influenced public opinion and protests against the war. It also touches upon the international relations and the role of coalition forces in the invasion, as well as the economic impact and reconstruction efforts post-Saddam Hussein.

In conclusion, "Sectarian Conflicts and Rise of Insurgency" offers a comprehensive analysis of the multifaceted relationship between the invasion and occupation of Iraq, sectarian conflicts, and the subsequent rise of insurgency. By examining these complexities, historians and those interested in Operation Iraqi Freedom can gain a deeper understanding of the legal aspects and controversies surrounding the invasion and occupation, as well as the broader implications for military strategy, political stability, and the well-being of both soldiers and civilians involved.

International Reactions and Diplomatic Challenges

The U.S.-led invasion of Iraq, known as Operation Iraqi Freedom, not only had immense military and political implications but also triggered a wave of international reactions and presented significant diplomatic challenges. The invasion, which aimed to remove Saddam Hussein from power and establish a more democratic regime in Iraq, was met with mixed responses from the international community.

While some countries, such as the United Kingdom and Australia, joined the coalition forces led by the United States and actively participated in the invasion, others, including France, Germany, and Russia, vehemently opposed the military action. These divisions within the international community strained diplomatic relations and posed challenges for the coalition forces during and after the invasion.

The opposition to the invasion was primarily based on concerns about the legality of the action, as it was carried out without explicit authorization from the United Nations Security Council. Critics argued that the invasion violated international law and undermined the authority of the United Nations. This legal controversy surrounding the invasion created a significant diplomatic hurdle for the coalition forces, as they had to justify their actions and maintain diplomatic relations with nations that opposed the invasion.

Furthermore, the invasion of Iraq led to strained relations with countries in the Middle East and the broader Muslim world. Many Arab nations, including traditional U.S. allies such as Saudi Arabia and Egypt, expressed their disapproval of the invasion. The perception that the invasion was driven by Western imperialism and a desire to control Iraq's oil resources fueled anti-American sentiment and strained diplomatic ties in the region.

The international community also had to grapple with the humanitarian consequences of the invasion. The military strategy and tactics employed during Operation Iraqi Freedom resulted in significant civilian casualties and displacement. These humanitarian challenges further exacerbated tensions between the coalition forces and the international community, with many countries criticizing the handling of the post-invasion reconstruction efforts and the failure to protect civilian lives adequately.

Moreover, the media coverage and propaganda surrounding Operation Iraqi Freedom played a crucial role in shaping international perceptions of the invasion. The media's portrayal of the war, both in the United States and abroad, influenced public opinion and fueled protests against the invasion in many countries. This public sentiment further complicated diplomatic efforts and strained relations between the coalition forces and the international community.

Overall, the international reactions and diplomatic challenges surrounding the U.S.-led invasion of Iraq were significant and multifaceted. The invasion triggered divisions within the international community, strained diplomatic relations, and sparked debates about the legality and legitimacy of the military action. The humanitarian consequences of the invasion, coupled with media coverage and public opinion, further complicated the international response to Operation Iraqi Freedom. Understanding these international reactions and diplomatic challenges is essential for historians studying the invasion and its aftermath, as it provides insights into the complex dynamics and controversies that surrounded this controversial chapter in history.

Transition to Iraqi Sovereignty

The transition to Iraqi sovereignty marked a crucial turning point in the tumultuous period following the U.S.-led invasion of Iraq and the removal of Saddam Hussein. This subchapter delves into the legal aspects and debates surrounding this transitional phase, shedding light on the complexities and controversies that arose during this transformative period.

From a legal perspective, the handover of power to the Iraqi people was a highly significant event. It signified the end of the occupation and the establishment of an Iraqi government that would determine the country's future. Historians studying Operation Iraqi Freedom will find this chapter particularly useful in understanding the legal framework within which this transition occurred.

This subchapter explores the political implications and aftermath of the invasion, providing historians with a comprehensive analysis of the evolving power dynamics in Iraq. It delves into the challenges faced by the newly formed Iraqi government, including the delicate balancing act of maintaining security and stability amidst ongoing violence and insurgency.

Another significant aspect covered in this subchapter is the humanitarian efforts and civilian casualties during the invasion and subsequent transition. Historians will gain insights into the immense challenges faced by humanitarian organizations in providing aid and assistance to the Iraqi people amidst the chaos and destruction.

The media coverage and propaganda surrounding Operation Iraqi Freedom are also addressed, offering historians a critical examination of how information was disseminated and manipulated during this period. The chapter explores the role of the media in shaping public opinion and the controversies surrounding the veracity of the information presented to the public.

Furthermore, this subchapter delves into the international relations and the role of coalition forces in the invasion. It examines the dynamics between the United States and its coalition partners, shedding light on the challenges faced in maintaining a united front and the differing motivations behind each country's involvement.

The hunt for weapons of mass destruction (WMDs) in Iraq and the role of intelligence are also explored in this subchapter. Historians will gain a deeper understanding of the intelligence failures and controversies surrounding the justification for the invasion.

Finally, this chapter touches upon the economic impact and reconstruction efforts post-Saddam Hussein. It provides an analysis of the challenges faced in rebuilding Iraq's infrastructure and economy amidst ongoing security concerns and political instability.

Overall, this subchapter offers historians a comprehensive exploration of the legal aspects and debates surrounding the transition to Iraqi sovereignty. It delves into the complexities and controversies that emerged during this period, providing valuable insights into the multifaceted nature of the invasion and occupation of Iraq.

Chapter 4: Humanitarian Efforts and Civilian Casualties during the Invasion

Protection of Civilians and Humanitarian Aid

The invasion and occupation of Iraq during Operation Iraqi Freedom had far-reaching consequences for both the Iraqi people and the international community. One of the key concerns during this period was the protection of civilians and the provision of humanitarian aid in the midst of conflict.

The U.S.-led invasion of Iraq witnessed a significant number of civilian casualties, leading to widespread criticism and concerns about the disregard for human life. Historians examining this chapter of history should not only focus on the military tactics employed but also on the ethical and legal implications of civilian deaths. The impact of these casualties on the Iraqi population cannot be underestimated, as innocent men, women, and children were caught in the crossfire and faced unimaginable suffering.

Humanitarian efforts played a crucial role in addressing the needs of the Iraqi people during and after the invasion. Despite the challenging circumstances, organizations such as the United Nations and various non-governmental organizations worked tirelessly to provide aid, medical assistance, and basic supplies to those affected by the conflict. These humanitarian endeavors, though often overlooked, were instrumental in alleviating the suffering of countless Iraqis.

However, access to vulnerable populations and the delivery of aid were hindered by the ongoing violence and insecurity. The military strategy and tactics employed during the invasion had a significant impact on the ability of humanitarian organizations to reach those in need. Historians must delve into the complexities of this relationship, examining how military operations and humanitarian efforts intersected and sometimes clashed.

The media coverage and propaganda surrounding Operation Iraqi Freedom also influenced the perception of humanitarian efforts and civilian casualties. Understanding the role of media in shaping public opinion is crucial for historians studying this period. The dissemination of accurate information and the uncovering of hidden truths are vital in order to fully comprehend the impact of the invasion and occupation on the Iraqi people.

Furthermore, the international relations and the role of coalition forces in the invasion shaped the extent and effectiveness of humanitarian aid. The collaboration between different nations and their commitment to providing assistance determined the success of these efforts. Historians should analyze the political implications of these alliances and the subsequent impact on the provision of aid to civilians.

Ultimately, the protection of civilians and the provision of humanitarian aid during Operation Iraqi Freedom remain critical aspects of the invasion and occupation of Iraq. Historians must examine the legal controversies, ethical dilemmas, and the long-lasting consequences in order to gain a comprehensive understanding of this complex chapter in history. By shedding light on these issues, they can help ensure that the mistakes and challenges faced during this period are not repeated in future military interventions.

Collateral Damage and Civilian Casualties

War is a brutal and unforgiving endeavor, and the invasion and occupation of Iraq during Operation Iraqi Freedom proved to be no exception. The subchapter "Collateral Damage and Civilian Casualties" delves into one of the most tragic aspects of this conflict, addressing the human cost of war.

Throughout the invasion, civilian casualties became an unavoidable consequence of the military strategy and tactics employed by the U.S.-led forces. The book explores how these casualties resulted from the use of air strikes, artillery bombardments, and ground operations. It analyzes the impact of these operations on Iraqi cities, towns, and villages, where innocent civilians found themselves caught in the crossfire.

Moreover, the subchapter delves into the ethical and legal implications of these civilian casualties. Historians will find a comprehensive examination of the rules of war, such as the principle of proportionality, which seeks to minimize harm to civilians. The book evaluates whether the U.S.-led forces adhered to these principles and investigates instances where they might have fallen short.

Beyond the immediate impact on civilian lives, the subchapter also explores the long-term consequences of the invasion. It examines the political aftermath and the implications of civilian casualties on the perception of the U.S.-led forces in Iraq and the international community. The book highlights how these casualties fueled anti-U.S. sentiment and protests, both within Iraq and across the globe.

In addition, the subchapter delves into the humanitarian efforts made during the invasion to mitigate civilian suffering. It examines the challenges faced by aid organizations and the efforts made to provide assistance and medical care to the affected population. The book analyzes the successes and failures of these humanitarian efforts and their impact on the overall perception of the invasion and occupation.

Drawing on extensive research and historical analysis, this subchapter presents a balanced and comprehensive account of the collateral damage and civilian casualties during Operation Iraqi Freedom. It offers a nuanced understanding of the human cost of war, shedding light on the often-overlooked aspects of conflict that have far-reaching implications for military strategy, international relations, and public opinion.

By examining this controversial and deeply human topic, historians and scholars will gain valuable insights into the complexities of modern warfare and the profound impact it has on the lives of civilians caught in its path.

Challenges in Providing Aid and Reconstruction

The invasion and occupation of Iraq, known as Operation Iraqi Freedom, not only brought about significant political and military changes but also posed immense challenges in providing aid and reconstruction in the war-torn country. This subchapter explores the multifaceted obstacles faced during the post-invasion period, shedding light on the complexities and controversies surrounding these efforts.

One of the primary challenges was the sheer scale of destruction caused by the invasion itself. The military strategy and tactics employed during Operation Iraqi Freedom, such as precision airstrikes and ground assaults, inevitably resulted in severe damage to infrastructure, including hospitals, schools, and vital utilities. This widespread destruction created a pressing need for immediate humanitarian aid and reconstruction efforts.

Another critical challenge was the political implications and aftermath of the U.S.-led invasion. The removal of Saddam Hussein's regime left a power vacuum, leading to a period of instability and sectarian violence. This volatile environment further complicated the delivery of aid and reconstruction as the safety of aid workers and the ability to coordinate efforts became increasingly challenging.

Moreover, the humanitarian efforts during the invasion were marred by civilian casualties. The significant use of force and the urban warfare tactics employed by both sides resulted in a high number of civilian deaths and injuries. This not only raised ethical concerns but also hindered the provision of aid, as the affected population became increasingly distrustful of foreign forces.

Media coverage and propaganda surrounding Operation Iraqi Freedom exacerbated the challenges faced in delivering aid and reconstruction. The narrative presented to the public, both domestically and internationally, influenced public opinion and shaped the perception of the conflict. This, in turn, impacted the willingness of nations and organizations to contribute resources and support to the reconstruction efforts.

Furthermore, the international relations and the role of coalition forces in the invasion added another layer of complexity to aid and reconstruction. The diverse composition of the coalition forces, each with its own objectives and interests, made coordination and decision-making a challenging endeavor. Additionally, the strained relations between the occupying forces and the Iraqi populace further hindered progress in reconstruction efforts.

Economic impact and reconstruction efforts post-Saddam Hussein were also significant challenges. The removal of the previous regime not only disrupted the existing economic infrastructure but also led to an increase in unemployment and poverty. Rebuilding the Iraqi economy and establishing sustainable development required substantial financial resources and long-term planning.

The psychological and emotional toll on soldiers and veterans of Operation Iraqi Freedom further complicated aid and reconstruction efforts. The trauma experienced by military personnel affected their ability to engage effectively in humanitarian activities, requiring additional support and resources.

Lastly, legal aspects and controversies surrounding the invasion and occupation of Iraq added another layer of complexity to providing aid and reconstruction. The legality of the invasion, the treatment of prisoners, and the responsibility for civilian casualties were among the key legal debates that influenced the provision of aid and the engagement of international organizations.

In conclusion, the challenges in providing aid and reconstruction in Iraq after the U.S.-led invasion were numerous and multifaceted. The scale of destruction, political instability, media coverage, international relations, economic impact, psychological toll on soldiers, and legal controversies all contributed to the complexities faced in rebuilding Iraq. Understanding these challenges is essential for historians examining the legacy of Operation Iraqi Freedom and its long-term implications.

Chapter 5: Media Coverage and Propaganda Surrounding Operation Iraqi Freedom

Role of Media in Shaping Public Perception

In the age of information, the role of media in shaping public perception cannot be understated. It serves as a powerful tool that not only disseminates news but also influences public opinion, particularly in times of war and conflict. This subchapter will delve into the significant role played by the media in shaping public perception during the U.S.-led invasion of Iraq, also known as Operation Iraqi Freedom.

The invasion of Iraq in 2003 was marked by intense media coverage, with news outlets providing real-time updates on the progress of the invasion. However, it soon became apparent that media coverage was not impartial but rather driven by various agendas. Journalists embedded with military units faced constraints and restrictions that hindered their ability to provide unbiased reporting. This raised questions about the credibility and objectivity of the information presented to the public.

Propaganda played a significant role in shaping public perception during Operation Iraqi Freedom. Governments on both sides of the conflict utilized media outlets as tools to further their own narratives. The U.S. government, in particular, employed sophisticated public relations techniques to bolster support for the invasion and occupation. This included the dissemination of misleading information about weapons of mass destruction, which later turned out to be non-existent. Such manipulation of the media distorted public perception and led to widespread support for the invasion.

Media coverage also played a crucial role in highlighting the humanitarian efforts and civilian casualties during the invasion. Images of destroyed infrastructure, injured civilians, and grieving families inundated news channels, evoking sympathy and raising questions about the legitimacy and morality of the invasion. These visuals contributed to the growing opposition to the war, both domestically and internationally.

Furthermore, the media's coverage of the psychological and emotional toll on soldiers and veterans of Operation Iraqi Freedom had a profound impact on public perception. Stories of post-traumatic stress disorder, physical injuries, and high suicide rates among veterans humanized the war and highlighted the cost paid by individuals serving in the military. This further fueled public debate and scrutiny of the U.S. government's decision to invade Iraq.

In conclusion, the media played a pivotal role in shaping public perception during the U.S.-led invasion of Iraq. However, it was not without controversy and bias. The manipulation of information, the dissemination of propaganda, and the constraints faced by journalists embedded with military units all influenced the public's understanding of the war. Understanding the role of media in shaping public perception is crucial in comprehending the complexities and controversies surrounding the invasion and occupation of Iraq.

Embedded Reporters and Access to Information

The role of embedded reporters in the invasion and occupation of Iraq is a topic that has generated significant controversy and debate. Embedded journalists are those who are attached to military units and have direct access to the frontlines, allowing them to report on the conflict in real-time. This subchapter explores the implications of embedded reporting on access to information during Operation Iraqi Freedom.

The decision to embed reporters with military units was seen as a way to provide the public with a firsthand account of the war. Supporters argued that embedded reporting would offer a balanced perspective and allow for a more accurate portrayal of the conflict. However, critics raised concerns about the potential for censorship and bias in the reporting process.

One of the key advantages of embedded reporting was the ability to gather immediate and detailed information about the situation on the ground. Reporters could witness battles, document the experiences of soldiers, and provide real-time updates to the public. This level of access allowed for a more nuanced understanding of the war, but it also raised questions about the objectivity of the reporting. Some argued that embedded reporters may become too reliant on the military for information, leading to a skewed perspective.

Another concern was the potential for censorship or self-censorship by embedded reporters. Critics argued that journalists embedded with military units might face pressure to present a favorable image of the war effort, leading to biased reporting. Additionally, the military had the power to restrict access to certain areas or information, limiting the ability of journalists to provide a comprehensive account of the conflict.

The impact of embedded reporting on the dissemination of information also extended to the broader media coverage of the war. The experiences and perspectives of embedded journalists often dominated the news cycle, overshadowing other significant aspects of the conflict. This resulted in a narrow focus on the military's perspective, while other critical dimensions such as civilian casualties, humanitarian efforts, and political implications received less attention.

In conclusion, embedded reporters played a significant role in shaping the narrative of Operation Iraqi Freedom. While they provided invaluable firsthand accounts of the conflict, their access to information was influenced by their attachment to military units, leading to potential biases and limitations. As historians, it is crucial to critically analyze the role of embedded reporters in understanding the complexities and controversies surrounding the invasion and occupation of Iraq.

Propaganda Techniques and Manipulation of Public Opinion

In the complex landscape of the invasion and occupation of Iraq, one cannot overlook the role that propaganda techniques played in shaping public opinion. This subchapter delves into the various methods employed to sway the masses and manipulate public sentiment during Operation Iraqi Freedom.

Propaganda, as a tool of psychological warfare, has long been used to control public opinion and mobilize support for military endeavors. This chapter examines the specific techniques employed by both the United States and its opponents, shedding light on the strategies employed to shape narratives and influence public perception.

The subchapter explores the utilization of fear, emotional appeals, and selective information dissemination as key propaganda techniques during the invasion and occupation of Iraq. It uncovers how these techniques were employed by both sides to rally support or sow doubt among the masses. Furthermore, it delves into the role of media manipulation and censorship in controlling the flow of information and shaping public opinion.

Moreover, this subchapter delves into the psychological impact of propaganda on soldiers and veterans of Operation Iraqi Freedom. It explores the emotional toll that exposure to propaganda can have on military personnel, examining the long-lasting effects on their mental well-being.

Drawing on historical records, media analysis, and expert opinions, this subchapter also explores the controversies surrounding the use of propaganda during the invasion and occupation of Iraq. It delves into the ethical implications of manipulating public opinion, particularly in a conflict that sparked significant debate and opposition.

By examining the propaganda techniques employed during Operation Iraqi Freedom, this subchapter offers historians a comprehensive understanding of the role of propaganda in shaping public opinion. It sheds light on the impact of these techniques on various aspects of the conflict, including military strategy, political implications, humanitarian efforts, and international relations.

With an emphasis on critical analysis and a multidisciplinary approach, this subchapter contributes to a nuanced understanding of the invasion and occupation of Iraq. It provides historians with invaluable insights into the power of propaganda and its lasting effects on public opinion and the overall narrative surrounding Operation Iraqi Freedom.

Critiques of Media Coverage and Controversies

In the fast-paced world of media, the coverage of Operation Iraqi Freedom has been a subject of intense scrutiny and criticism. Historians, who meticulously analyze events to provide an accurate account of history, have identified numerous flaws and controversies surrounding the media's portrayal of the invasion and occupation of Iraq. This subchapter examines some of the key critiques and controversies surrounding media coverage during this period.

One of the most significant criticisms relates to the presence of propaganda during Operation Iraqi Freedom. Historians argue that media outlets, both in the United States and internationally, were influenced by political agendas and biases. This led to a distortion of the facts and a failure to provide an objective account of events. The media's unquestioning acceptance of the Bush administration's claims about weapons of mass destruction in Iraq is a prime example of this bias.

It is now widely acknowledged that these claims were based on faulty intelligence, yet the media failed to critically examine them at the time.

Another critique centers around the sensationalism and lack of context in media coverage. The invasion and occupation of Iraq were complex and multifaceted, but the media often focused on dramatic events and simplistic narratives. This resulted in a superficial understanding of the conflict and a failure to adequately inform the public about the complexities and nuances of the situation on the ground.

Furthermore, there were concerns about the media's role in shaping public opinion and stifling dissent. Some historians argue that the media's uncritical support for the war effort contributed to a climate of nationalism and suppressed alternative viewpoints. This limited the scope of public debate and hindered a more comprehensive understanding of the consequences of the invasion.

Additionally, media coverage of civilian casualties and humanitarian efforts during the invasion has been a subject of controversy. Critics argue that the media often failed to provide a comprehensive account of the human cost of the conflict, focusing instead on military successes and strategic objectives. This skewed portrayal overlooked the suffering endured by Iraqi civilians and hindered efforts to address their needs.

Overall, the critiques of media coverage and controversies surrounding Operation Iraqi Freedom highlight the need for a more critical and comprehensive approach to reporting on war. Historians play a vital role in analyzing and interpreting these events, ensuring that future generations have an accurate understanding of the complexities and implications of the invasion and occupation of Iraq. By examining these critiques, historians can shed light on the shortcomings of media coverage and contribute to a more nuanced understanding of this significant chapter in history.

Chapter 6: International Relations and the Role of Coalition Forces in the Invasion

Coalition Building and Multinational Efforts

In the subchapter "Coalition Building and Multinational Efforts," we delve into the intricate web of alliances and the collective military, political, and humanitarian efforts that shaped the U.S.-led invasion of Iraq. This chapter explores the role of coalition forces, the intricacies of international relations, and the controversies surrounding their involvement.

The U.S.-led invasion of Iraq, known as Operation Iraqi Freedom, was not a solo venture. It relied heavily on coalition forces from various countries, each with their own unique motivations and objectives. Historians interested in understanding the complexities of this military operation will find this subchapter enlightening.

Coalition building played a crucial role in garnering international support for the invasion. The chapter examines the motivations behind countries joining the coalition, such as their strategic interests, concerns over Saddam Hussein's regime, or the desire to strengthen ties with the United States. It also analyzes the challenges faced in maintaining this coalition, including diverging interests and the impact of public opinion on participating nations.

Multinational efforts extended beyond the military aspect. The chapter delves into the humanitarian efforts and civilian casualties during the invasion. It explores the challenges faced by coalition forces in distinguishing combatants from non-combatants and the impact of these operations on the Iraqi population. By examining these aspects, historians gain a comprehensive understanding of the invasion's consequences on both military objectives and civilian lives.

Furthermore, the role of intelligence and the hunt for weapons of mass destruction (WMDs) is discussed. This subchapter critically analyzes the intelligence failures and controversies surrounding the justification for the invasion based on the presence of WMDs. It explores the impact of flawed intelligence on the coalition's objectives and public opinion, shedding light on the complexities of decision-making during this period.

The subchapter also delves into the political implications and aftermath of the U.S.-led invasion, including the challenges faced during post-Saddam Hussein reconstruction efforts and the economic impact on Iraq. It addresses the psychological and emotional toll on soldiers and veterans of Operation Iraqi Freedom, offering valuable insights into the human cost of war.

By exploring the media coverage and propaganda surrounding Operation Iraqi Freedom, this subchapter highlights the role of the media in shaping public opinion and the controversies surrounding information dissemination during the invasion and occupation. It also explores the legal aspects and controversies surrounding the invasion and occupation of Iraq, shedding light on the complex legal framework underpinning this military operation.

Overall, "Coalition Building and Multinational Efforts" provides historians with a comprehensive analysis of the international dynamics, military strategy, political implications, and humanitarian efforts that shaped the U.S.-led invasion of Iraq. This subchapter offers invaluable insights into the multifaceted nature of Operation Iraqi Freedom and its far-reaching consequences.

Role of NATO and Non-NATO Allies

The Role of NATO and Non-NATO Allies

In the tumultuous landscape of the U.S.-led invasion of Iraq and the subsequent occupation, the role of NATO and non-NATO allies played a significant part in shaping the outcome of Operation Iraqi Freedom. This subchapter aims to illuminate the various aspects of their involvement, exploring the legal, political, and military implications that arose during this controversial period in history.

NATO, as an alliance based on collective defense, faced a crucial test in deciding its stance on the invasion of Iraq. While some member countries, such as the United States, the United Kingdom, and Poland, actively participated in the invasion, others, including France and Germany, strongly opposed it. This divergence within the alliance highlighted the complexities of transatlantic relations and raised questions about the future of NATO's unity.

Non-NATO allies, such as Australia and Japan, also played a pivotal role in Operation Iraqi Freedom. These countries provided military support to the U.S.-led coalition, reinforcing the notion that the invasion was not solely an American endeavor. Their involvement brought international legitimacy to the mission, but also sparked debates about the extent of their contributions and the implications of their participation.

From a military perspective, the inclusion of NATO and non-NATO allies brought diverse capabilities to the coalition forces. The experiences, strategies, and tactics of these nations varied significantly, leading to challenges in coordination and integration. However, their combined efforts proved instrumental in achieving certain military objectives, such as the removal of Saddam Hussein's regime.

Politically, the involvement of NATO and non-NATO allies had ramifications that extended beyond the borders of Iraq. The alliance's divisions strained relations between member countries, triggering debates about the future of NATO's role and its ability to respond collectively to emerging security threats. The participation of non-NATO allies also raised questions about the role of non-state actors in international affairs and the extent to which their contributions should be recognized.

The legal aspects surrounding the invasion and occupation of Iraq became ever more complex with the involvement of NATO and non-NATO allies. The justifications for military intervention, the authorization from the United Nations, and the adherence to international law were all subject to scrutiny and controversy. The diverse legal frameworks of the different nations involved further complicated matters, highlighting the need for a comprehensive understanding of the legal implications of multinational military operations.

The role of NATO and non-NATO allies in Operation Iraqi Freedom cannot be understated. Their involvement shaped the trajectory of the invasion and subsequent occupation, influencing military strategies, political dynamics, legal debates, and international relations. As historians reflecting on this period, it is essential to analyze the multifaceted roles played by these actors and their impact on the broader context of the invasion and occupation of Iraq.

Challenges in Coordinating International Forces

The invasion and occupation of Iraq during Operation Iraqi Freedom involved a complex web of international forces, each with their own objectives, strategies, and political considerations. Coordinating these forces presented numerous challenges that impacted the overall success and effectiveness of the mission. This subchapter explores the key obstacles faced in coordinating international forces and the implications they had on the invasion and subsequent occupation.

One of the primary challenges in coordinating international forces was the stark divergence in military strategies and tactics. The United States, as the leading force, had a clear vision and approach to the operation, while other coalition partners brought their own perspectives and priorities. The lack of unified military strategy resulted in coordination difficulties, communication breakdowns, and even conflicting objectives on the battlefield. This challenge was particularly pronounced in urban warfare scenarios where the need for precise coordination was crucial.

Another challenge stemmed from the political implications and aftermath of the U.S.-led invasion. Many coalition partners faced public backlash and domestic political debates regarding their involvement in the conflict. This led to wavering commitment, changes in deployment schedules, and even early withdrawals by some nations. These political factors further complicated the coordination efforts and strained the cohesion of the international coalition.

Furthermore, the humanitarian efforts and civilian casualties during the invasion posed significant challenges. Coordinating international forces to minimize civilian harm while targeting legitimate military objectives required extensive coordination, cultural understanding, and adherence to international humanitarian law. However, the complexities of urban warfare, where civilians and combatants often intermingled, made it difficult to avoid collateral damage. These challenges strained the coordination between international forces and raised ethical questions about the proportionality of military actions.

Additionally, media coverage and propaganda surrounding Operation Iraqi Freedom presented challenges in coordinating international forces. Each nation had its own media narratives, which often influenced public opinion and shaped political decisions. The divergence in media coverage impacted the perception of the mission's legitimacy and success, thereby affecting the coordination and unity among international forces.

The role of intelligence and the hunt for weapons of mass destruction in Iraq also posed coordination challenges. Different nations had varying levels of access to intelligence and often pursued different lines of investigation. This lack of intelligence sharing hindered the effectiveness of coordinated operations and limited the success of the mission.

In conclusion, coordinating international forces during Operation Iraqi Freedom presented numerous challenges with significant implications. These challenges included divergent military strategies, political considerations, humanitarian concerns, media narratives, intelligence sharing, and more. Understanding and addressing these challenges is crucial for historians studying the invasion and occupation of Iraq, as they shaped the overall effectiveness and outcomes of the mission.

Long-term Implications for International Relations

The invasion and occupation of Iraq, commonly referred to as Operation Iraqi Freedom, have had far-reaching consequences for international relations. This subchapter delves into the lasting impact of this controversial military intervention and its aftermath, examining the various dimensions that have shaped the global landscape.

One of the most significant long-term implications of the U.S.-led invasion of Iraq is the erosion of trust and credibility in international relations. The decision to invade Iraq without clear evidence of weapons of mass destruction strained alliances and undermined the credibility of intelligence agencies. This has led to a cautious approach from other nations when collaborating with the United States on matters of international security, with a greater emphasis on independent verification.

Furthermore, the invasion highlighted the limitations of military strategy and tactics in achieving long-term stability. The failure to adequately plan for the post-invasion phase resulted in a power vacuum and the rise of various insurgent groups. This has reshaped military doctrines, emphasizing the need for comprehensive strategies that consider the political, social, and economic dimensions of conflict resolution.

The political implications and aftermath of the invasion have also had a profound impact on international relations. The removal of Saddam Hussein destabilized the region and sparked sectarian tensions, leading to a rise in extremist ideologies. This, in turn, has fueled conflicts across the Middle East and created a breeding ground for the emergence of terrorist organizations such as ISIS.

Humanitarian efforts and civilian casualties during the invasion have further strained international relations. The high number of civilian deaths and the destruction of infrastructure have garnered global condemnation, undermining the legitimacy of the invasion. The international community has been forced to grapple with the ethical implications of military interventions and the responsibility to protect civilian populations in times of conflict.

Additionally, the media coverage and propaganda surrounding Operation Iraqi Freedom have had a lasting impact on public perception and international relations. The dissemination of misinformation and the manipulation of public opinion have deepened distrust and skepticism towards media narratives. This has heightened the importance of critical thinking and independent analysis in assessing global events.

The role of coalition forces in the invasion has also shaped international relations. The participation of various nations in the coalition has strained diplomatic relations and raised questions about their motivations and interests. The invasion has highlighted the complexities of multilateral military operations and the challenges of maintaining cohesion among diverse allies.

Economically, the invasion and subsequent reconstruction efforts have had significant implications for global markets. The cost of the war, coupled with the mismanagement of funds, has strained the U.S. economy and contributed to the global financial crisis of 2008. The reconstruction efforts have also raised questions about the role of international actors in rebuilding war-torn nations and the responsibility to provide aid and support.

Finally, the psychological and emotional toll on soldiers and veterans of Operation Iraqi Freedom has raised awareness about the long-term impact of war on individuals and societies. This has sparked discussions about the provision of adequate support and resources for veterans and the need to address the hidden costs of military interventions.

In conclusion, the invasion and occupation of Iraq have had far-reaching implications for international relations. From the erosion of trust and credibility to the reshaping of military strategies, the consequences of this controversial intervention continue to reverberate globally. Understanding these long-term implications is crucial for historians and those interested in the complexities of international relations in the post-9/11 era.

Chapter 7: The Role of Intelligence and the Hunt for Weapons of Mass Destruction in Iraq

Intelligence Reports and Justification for Invasion

The subchapter "Intelligence Reports and Justification for Invasion" delves into the crucial role that intelligence played in the decision-making process leading up to the U.S.-led invasion of Iraq and the subsequent removal of Saddam Hussein. Addressing the audience of historians and various niches within the broader topic of Operation Iraqi Freedom, this chapter aims to provide a comprehensive analysis of the intelligence gathered, its impact on the military strategy, political implications, and aftermath of the invasion.

This subchapter explores how intelligence reports formed the basis for the justification of the invasion. It delves into the alleged existence of weapons of mass destruction (WMDs) in Iraq and how this claim influenced the decision-making process. The chapter scrutinizes the reliability of the intelligence sources, the accuracy of the information provided, and the subsequent controversies surrounding the failure to find substantial evidence of WMDs.

Furthermore, this subchapter sheds light on how intelligence reports influenced military strategy and tactics during Operation Iraqi Freedom. It examines how the military relied on intelligence to identify targets, plan operations, and assess potential threats. It analyzes the successes and failures of intelligence in providing accurate and timely information to the military commanders on the ground.

Additionally, the chapter addresses the political implications and aftermath of the invasion, highlighting the impact that flawed intelligence and the failure to find WMDs had on the credibility of the

U.S. government. It explores how the reliance on faulty intelligence led to a loss of public trust, both domestically and internationally, and fueled anti-war sentiments and protests.

Moreover, this subchapter discusses the humanitarian efforts and civilian casualties during the invasion, emphasizing the importance of accurate intelligence in minimizing collateral damage and protecting innocent lives. It also examines the media coverage and propaganda surrounding Operation Iraqi Freedom, exploring how intelligence reports were presented to the public and how they influenced public opinion.

Furthermore, the subchapter touches on the international relations and the role of coalition forces in the invasion, highlighting how intelligence sharing and cooperation among different nations influenced the outcome. It also delves into the economic impact and reconstruction efforts post-Saddam Hussein, discussing how intelligence played a role in identifying priorities and guiding the reconstruction process.

Lastly, the subchapter examines the psychological and emotional toll on soldiers and veterans of Operation Iraqi Freedom, emphasizing the importance of intelligence in understanding the enemy and mitigating the long-term effects of combat trauma.

Overall, this subchapter provides a comprehensive analysis of the role of intelligence in the invasion of Iraq, addressing its impact on various aspects such as military strategy, political implications, humanitarian efforts, media coverage, international relations, economic impact, and the well-being of soldiers. Through a critical examination of intelligence reports and their subsequent justifications, this chapter offers historians and other interested readers a nuanced understanding of the complexities and controversies surrounding the invasion and occupation of Iraq.

Failure to Find Weapons of Mass Destruction

One of the most controversial aspects of the U.S.-led invasion of Iraq was the failure to find weapons of mass destruction (WMDs) that were cited as a primary justification for the military action. This subchapter delves into the numerous implications and debates surrounding this failure, providing a comprehensive analysis of the various factors involved.

The hunt for WMDs in Iraq was a critical objective for the coalition forces during the invasion. However, despite extensive efforts and intelligence reports suggesting their existence, no substantial evidence was found. This failure raised serious questions about the credibility of the intelligence that led to the invasion in the first place, as well as the decision-making process within the U.S. government.

For historians studying Operation Iraqi Freedom, the failure to find WMDs serves as a case study in the flaws of intelligence gathering and the potential for misinformation. It highlights the complexities of relying on intelligence reports and the need for critical analysis before launching military operations. Moreover, it raises ethical concerns about the justifications used to wage war, specifically the manipulation of intelligence to garner public support.

Furthermore, the failure to find WMDs had far-reaching political implications and contributed to the erosion of public trust in the U.S. government and its allies. This subchapter examines how this failure affected the domestic and international political landscape, leading to increased skepticism of U.S. foreign policy and triggering widespread protests against Operation Iraqi Freedom.

Additionally, the absence of WMDs had a profound impact on the humanitarian efforts and civilian casualties during the invasion. The belief that Saddam Hussein possessed WMDs justified the invasion as a preventive measure, but the absence of these weapons called into question the legitimacy of the military action and the resulting civilian deaths.

Moreover, media coverage and propaganda surrounding Operation Iraqi Freedom played a significant role in shaping public opinion. This subchapter explores how the failure to find WMDs influenced media narratives and the subsequent impact on public perception and support for the war.

Ultimately, the failure to find WMDs had profound consequences for the invasion and occupation of Iraq. It raised critical questions about the role of intelligence, the credibility of justifications for war, and the long-term implications for international relations. By analyzing this controversial aspect, historians gain valuable insights into the multifaceted nature of the invasion and its aftermath.

Intelligence Failures and Implications for Future Operations

In the subchapter "Intelligence Failures and Implications for Future Operations," we delve into one of the most critical aspects of the U.S.-led invasion of Iraq: the role of intelligence and the hunt for weapons of mass destruction (WMDs). This topic is of great significance to historians studying Operation Iraqi Freedom, as it sheds light on the decision-making process and the lessons learned from these failures.

The invasion of Iraq in 2003 was primarily justified by claims that Saddam Hussein possessed WMDs, which posed a threat to regional and global security. However, as subsequent investigations revealed, these claims were based on faulty intelligence, misinterpretations, and unreliable sources. This intelligence failure had far-reaching implications, shaping the course of the invasion and its aftermath.

First and foremost, the reliance on faulty intelligence undermined the legitimacy of the invasion in the eyes of the international community and the public. The lack of concrete evidence eroded the credibility of the coalition forces and created a perception of a rushed and ill-informed decision. This, in turn, fueled protests, both within the United States and globally, against Operation Iraqi Freedom.

Furthermore, the intelligence failures had severe consequences for military strategy and tactics during the invasion. The inaccurate information led to misguided targeting decisions and a miscalculation of the enemy's capabilities, resulting in unnecessary casualties for both military personnel and civilians. These failures highlighted the need for greater scrutiny and verification of intelligence reports in future military operations.

The implications of these intelligence failures extended beyond the invasion phase. The failure to find WMDs undermined the credibility of the U.S. government and its allies, raising questions about their motivations and the true reasons behind the invasion. This, in turn, had political implications, both domestically and internationally, as it fueled skepticism and mistrust towards the U.S.-led coalition.

From a broader perspective, the intelligence failures in Iraq serve as a cautionary tale for future military operations. They underscore the importance of robust and reliable intelligence, as well as the need for thorough analysis and verification of information before making critical decisions. The lessons learned from these failures have since informed and shaped intelligence practices, ensuring that similar mistakes are not repeated in future conflicts.

In conclusion, the intelligence failures and their implications for future operations are a crucial aspect of understanding the invasion and occupation of Iraq. Historians studying Operation Iraqi Freedom must acknowledge and analyze these failures to gain a comprehensive understanding of the decision-making process, the consequences of faulty intelligence, and the lessons learned for future military endeavors.

Accountability and Oversight of Intelligence Agencies

In the subchapter "Accountability and Oversight of Intelligence Agencies," we delve into one of the most critical aspects of the invasion and occupation of Iraq – the role of intelligence and the subsequent hunt for weapons of mass destruction (WMDs). As historians, it is crucial for us to examine the accountability and oversight mechanisms in place to ensure the accuracy and reliability of intelligence reports, thereby avoiding the disastrous consequences of misinformation.

The intelligence agencies involved in the lead-up to Operation Iraqi Freedom, such as the CIA and MI6, played a pivotal role in shaping the decision-making process of world leaders. However, the subsequent failure to discover WMDs in Iraq raises serious questions about the reliability of the intelligence provided.

This subchapter critically analyzes the accountability mechanisms within intelligence agencies and the oversight of their activities. It examines the extent to which these agencies were held responsible for the faulty information they provided, which ultimately led to the invasion of Iraq. We explore how the intelligence community, both in the United States and the United Kingdom, conducted investigations and implemented reforms to prevent such failures in the future.

Furthermore, we shed light on the role of congressional committees and parliamentary inquiries in holding intelligence agencies accountable. By delving into the actions taken by these bodies to investigate the accuracy and credibility of the intelligence reports, we gain a deeper understanding of the checks and balances within the intelligence community.

Additionally, we explore the legal aspects and controversies surrounding the invasion and occupation of Iraq, examining how the lack of accountability and oversight of intelligence agencies influenced the decision-making process. By analyzing the legal frameworks in place at the time, we evaluate whether the actions taken by intelligence agencies were within the bounds of international law.

Ultimately, this subchapter provides historians with a comprehensive overview of the accountability and oversight mechanisms surrounding intelligence agencies during the invasion and occupation of Iraq. By examining the failures and subsequent reforms, we gain valuable insights into the importance of transparency and accuracy in intelligence gathering, and the consequences that can arise from its absence.

Chapter 8: Economic Impact and Reconstruction Efforts Post-Saddam Hussein

Challenges in Rebuilding Infrastructure and Economy

The invasion and occupation of Iraq by the United States during Operation Iraqi Freedom had far-reaching consequences, particularly in terms of the challenges faced in rebuilding the country's infrastructure and economy. In this subchapter, we will explore the various obstacles encountered in this process and their implications for the future of Iraq.

One of the primary challenges in rebuilding Iraq's infrastructure was the extensive damage caused by the military operations. The invasion led to the destruction of vital infrastructure such as roads, bridges, power plants, and water treatment facilities. These damages severely hampered the provision of basic services to the Iraqi population and hindered efforts to kickstart the economy.

Another significant challenge was the lack of local capacity and expertise. Decades of underinvestment and neglect under Saddam Hussein's regime left Iraq ill-prepared to undertake large-scale reconstruction projects. The country faced a shortage of skilled labor, engineers, and professionals necessary to rebuild its infrastructure effectively. Furthermore, the brain drain caused by the exodus of intellectuals during the invasion further exacerbated this problem.

The security situation in post-invasion Iraq posed a major obstacle to reconstruction efforts. Insurgent attacks, sectarian violence, and the rise of various armed factions created an environment of instability and insecurity. This made it difficult for international organizations, contractors, and investors to operate effectively, further impeding the progress of reconstruction projects.

Financial constraints also presented a significant challenge. The cost of rebuilding Iraq after years of war and sanctions was daunting. The U.S. government initially allocated billions of dollars for reconstruction, but mismanagement and corruption hindered the efficient use of these funds. Additionally, the global economic recession and falling oil prices further strained Iraq's financial resources, limiting its ability to invest in reconstruction projects.

The lack of coordination and cooperation among different actors involved in the reconstruction process was yet another challenge. Multiple international organizations, NGOs, and military forces were involved in various aspects of rebuilding Iraq, but their efforts were often fragmented and uncoordinated. This lack of synergy resulted in duplication of efforts, inefficiencies, and wasted resources.

In conclusion, the challenges faced in rebuilding Iraq's infrastructure and economy after the U.S.-led invasion were multifaceted and complex. The destruction caused by the invasion, the lack of local capacity, the security situation, financial constraints, and the lack of coordination all posed significant hurdles to the reconstruction process. Understanding these challenges is crucial for historians studying the aftermath of Operation Iraqi Freedom and for informing future approaches to post-conflict reconstruction.

Role of International Aid and Investment

Title: Role of International Aid and Investment in the Invasion and Occupation of Iraq

Introduction:

The role of international aid and investment in the invasion and occupation of Iraq has been a subject of great controversy and debate. This subchapter aims to explore the various aspects and implications of international aid and investment in the context of Operation Iraqi

Freedom. By analyzing the economic impact, humanitarian efforts, and reconstruction efforts post-Saddam Hussein, this chapter sheds light on the complex dynamics between international actors and the invaded nation.

Economic Impact:

International aid and investment played a crucial role in shaping Iraq's economic landscape post-Saddam Hussein. While the invasion caused significant damage to the country's infrastructure and economy, foreign assistance aimed to rebuild and stabilize the nation. Despite the noble intentions, the economic impact of international aid and investment remains a contentious issue, with debates centering around the distribution of funds, corruption, and the effectiveness of economic reforms.

Humanitarian Efforts and Civilian Casualties:

The invasion of Iraq resulted in significant civilian casualties and displacement. International aid organizations and humanitarian efforts played a pivotal role in providing assistance to those affected by the conflict. However, controversies arose regarding the adequacy of aid and the ability of international actors to address the growing humanitarian crisis. The subchapter delves into the challenges faced by aid organizations and the long-term consequences for the Iraqi civilian population.

Reconstruction Efforts Post-Saddam Hussein:

The reconstruction of Iraq post-Saddam Hussein was a massive undertaking that required substantial international aid and investment. This section examines the various reconstruction projects initiated by international actors, ranging from rebuilding infrastructure to establishing democratic institutions. The chapter highlights the successes and failures of reconstruction efforts, exploring the impact on Iraq's political and social landscape.

International Relations and Coalition Forces:

International aid and investment were closely intertwined with the role of coalition forces during the invasion and occupation of Iraq. This section delves into the complex dynamics between international actors and the invaded nation, analyzing the motivations behind foreign involvement and the implications for Iraq's sovereignty.

Conclusion:

The role of international aid and investment in the invasion and occupation of Iraq was multifaceted, with both positive and negative consequences. While foreign assistance aimed to rebuild and stabilize Iraq, controversies regarding the economic impact, humanitarian efforts, and reconstruction initiatives persist. Understanding the complexities surrounding international aid and investment is essential for historians and scholars studying Operation Iraqi Freedom and its aftermath. By critically examining these aspects, a more comprehensive analysis of the invasion and occupation of Iraq can be achieved.

Corruption and Mismanagement in Reconstruction Efforts

The reconstruction efforts in Iraq following the U.S.-led invasion and the removal of Saddam Hussein were marred by rampant corruption and mismanagement. This subchapter delves into the various instances of corruption and mismanagement that plagued the post-war reconstruction, shedding light on the legal aspects and debates surrounding them.

One of the major issues that emerged during the reconstruction phase was the awarding of contracts to private companies, many of which had close ties to U.S. officials and lacked experience in reconstruction projects. This led to inflated costs, shoddy workmanship, and delays in completing crucial infrastructure projects. The lack of proper oversight and accountability mechanisms allowed corruption to flourish, with contractors pocketing huge sums of money without delivering the promised results.

Mismanagement also plagued the reconstruction efforts, with various government agencies and departments failing to coordinate effectively. This lack of coordination resulted in duplication of efforts, wasted resources, and inefficient allocation of funds. Additionally, the absence of a clear and comprehensive plan for reconstruction hampered progress and hindered the effective utilization of available resources.

The mismanagement and corruption in reconstruction efforts had severe consequences on the ground. Basic services such as electricity, water, and healthcare remained inadequate for the local population, exacerbating their already dire living conditions. Moreover, the lack of progress in rebuilding infrastructure and restoring essential services fueled resentment and distrust among Iraqis, further complicating the stabilization process.

From a legal standpoint, the subchapter explores the controversies surrounding the awarding of contracts and the accountability of those involved in corrupt practices. It delves into the legal frameworks in place to prevent corruption and mismanagement, analyzing their effectiveness and highlighting the challenges faced in their implementation.

For historians studying the invasion and occupation of Iraq, understanding the extent and impact of corruption and mismanagement in reconstruction efforts is crucial. It provides insights into the challenges faced by the occupying forces, the difficulties encountered in stabilizing the country, and the long-term implications for Iraq's future.

Ultimately, this subchapter sheds light on the complex web of corruption and mismanagement that plagued the reconstruction efforts in Iraq. By examining the legal aspects and controversies surrounding these issues, historians can gain a comprehensive understanding of the challenges faced during the post-war reconstruction period and draw lessons for future operations.

Long-term Economic Consequences and Opportunities

In the aftermath of the U.S.-led invasion of Iraq and the removal of Saddam Hussein, the long-term economic consequences and opportunities emerged as significant aspects to be examined. This subchapter aims to shed light on the various dimensions of the economic impact and reconstruction efforts post-Saddam Hussein, providing historians with a comprehensive understanding of this crucial aspect of the invasion and occupation of Iraq.

The economic aftermath of the invasion presented both challenges and opportunities for Iraq. On one hand, the country faced substantial damage to its infrastructure, including oil refineries, power plants, and transportation networks. This destruction hindered the immediate recovery of the Iraqi economy and posed significant challenges to the provision of basic services to its population. The subsequent years witnessed efforts to rebuild and rehabilitate these essential sectors, aiming to restore economic stability and improve the living conditions of Iraqis.

The reconstruction efforts in Iraq also provided numerous opportunities for foreign companies, particularly those from the United States. These companies were eager to participate in the restoration of Iraq's infrastructure and the development of its oil industry. Contracts worth billions of dollars were awarded to foreign firms, creating new economic ties between Iraq and the international community. However, this economic involvement brought its own set of controversies and debates, with many questioning the fairness and transparency of the contracting processes.

Moreover, the economic impact of the invasion extended beyond the physical reconstruction efforts. The removal of Saddam Hussein's regime created a power vacuum that led to a surge in corruption and the emergence of illicit economic activities. Historians should explore the consequences of this environment on Iraq's economy, as well as the efforts made to combat corruption and establish transparent governance structures.

Additionally, the economic impact of the invasion had broader regional implications. The invasion disrupted the stability of the Middle East, leading to increased oil prices and global economic uncertainties. These consequences reverberated beyond Iraq's borders, shaping international relations and affecting the economies of neighboring countries.

By examining the long-term economic consequences and opportunities, historians can gain a comprehensive understanding of the invasion and occupation of Iraq. This subchapter provides valuable insights into the challenges faced by Iraq in rebuilding its infrastructure, the controversies surrounding the economic involvement of foreign companies, and the broader regional implications of the invasion. It also offers a glimpse into the economic landscape that shaped the post-Saddam Hussein era and influenced the lives of millions of Iraqis.

Chapter 9: Psychological and Emotional Toll on Soldiers and Veterans of Operation Iraqi Freedom

Deployment and Combat Stress

One of the often overlooked aspects of war is the psychological toll it takes on the soldiers involved. In the case of the U.S.-led invasion of Iraq, known as Operation Iraqi Freedom, the deployment and combat stress experienced by soldiers was a significant issue that impacted both their mental and physical well-being.

The deployment process itself was a source of stress for many soldiers. Leaving behind their families and familiar surroundings, they were thrust into a foreign and hostile environment. The uncertainty of the mission, the constant threat of danger, and the high stakes involved all contributed to a heightened sense of anxiety and stress among the troops.

Once deployed, soldiers faced the realities of combat stress. The constant exposure to violence, death, and destruction took a toll on their mental health. Many experienced symptoms of post-traumatic stress disorder (PTSD), including flashbacks, nightmares, and hypervigilance. The stress of combat also manifested physically, with soldiers suffering from insomnia, headaches, and gastrointestinal issues.

The long deployments and extended periods of combat further exacerbated the stress levels. Soldiers were often under immense pressure to perform, leading to a constant state of alertness and hyperarousal. The fear of making a mistake or letting down their comrades added to the psychological burden they carried.

Additionally, the lack of support for mental health issues and the stigma associated with seeking help only intensified the problem. Many soldiers felt compelled to keep their feelings hidden, fearing that admitting to psychological distress would be seen as a sign of weakness.

The consequences of deployment and combat stress were far-reaching. Not only did it impact the soldiers themselves, but it also affected their relationships with their families and loved ones. The strain of war, combined with the psychological toll it took on soldiers, often resulted in broken families, divorce, and even suicide.

Recognizing the importance of addressing this issue, efforts were made to improve mental health support for soldiers during and after Operation Iraqi Freedom. However, the long-lasting effects of deployment and combat stress continue to be felt by many veterans to this day.

In conclusion, the deployment and combat stress experienced by soldiers during Operation Iraqi Freedom had a profound impact on their mental and physical well-being. The psychological toll of war, including symptoms of PTSD and the strain on relationships, cannot be understated. It is crucial for historians and those interested in the U.S.-led invasion of Iraq to acknowledge the psychological and emotional toll on soldiers and veterans and to understand the long-lasting effects it has had on their lives.

Post-Traumatic Stress Disorder (PTSD) and Mental Health Issues

The invasion and occupation of Iraq, known as Operation Iraqi Freedom, had far-reaching consequences that extended beyond the political and military realms. One of the most significant but often overlooked aspects of this conflict is the psychological and emotional toll it inflicted on soldiers and veterans. Post-Traumatic Stress Disorder (PTSD) and other mental health issues emerged as a significant concern for those who served in Iraq, and understanding the impact of these conditions is essential for historians studying this period.

The experiences of soldiers during the Iraq War were marked by extreme stress, constant danger, and the witnessing of horrifying events. These factors, combined with the prolonged and intense nature of the conflict, contributed to the development of PTSD among many military personnel. Symptoms of PTSD can include intrusive memories, nightmares, flashbacks, hypervigilance, and emotional numbness. These symptoms can significantly impair an individual's ability to function in their daily lives and have a long-lasting impact on their mental well-being.

Moreover, the prevalence of mental health issues extended beyond PTSD. Depression, anxiety, substance abuse, and suicidal ideation were also common among veterans. These conditions often arose due to the trauma experienced during deployment, difficulties reintegrating into civilian life, and the lack of appropriate support systems. The mental health of soldiers and veterans became an important concern, not just during the conflict but also in the years following their return home.

The consequences of these mental health issues extended beyond the individual level. The strain on families, communities, and healthcare systems cannot be understated. Historians studying Operation Iraqi Freedom must consider the broader implications of these mental health challenges and their impact on society as a whole.

Understanding the psychological and emotional toll on soldiers and veterans is crucial for comprehending the full scope of the invasion and occupation of Iraq. By examining the experiences of those who served, historians can shed light on the complexities of war and its lasting effects on individuals and societies. Moreover, this understanding can inform future military strategies, policies, and support systems to better address the mental health needs of those who serve their countries in times of conflict.

In conclusion, the mental health issues, particularly PTSD, that arose as a result of the invasion and occupation of Iraq are a critical aspect of the history of Operation Iraqi Freedom. Historians must delve into the experiences of soldiers and veterans to gain a comprehensive understanding of the conflict's long-lasting impact. By acknowledging and addressing these mental health challenges, societies can better support those who sacrifice their well-being for their nations.

Support Systems for Soldiers and Veterans

Operation Iraqi Freedom, the U.S.-led invasion of Iraq and the subsequent occupation, had a profound impact on the lives of soldiers and veterans who served in this conflict. The physical, psychological, and emotional toll on these individuals cannot be overstated. In this subchapter, we will delve into the support systems that were put in place to assist soldiers and veterans in coping with the challenges they faced during and after the invasion.

One of the key aspects of support for soldiers and veterans was the provision of healthcare services. The U.S. Department of Veterans Affairs (VA) played a crucial role in ensuring that soldiers and veterans had access to comprehensive medical care. This included physical rehabilitation, mental health services, and assistance with conditions such as post-traumatic stress disorder (PTSD). The VA also provided support for families of soldiers and veterans, recognizing the importance of a holistic approach to their well-being.

Additionally, numerous non-profit organizations emerged to provide additional support and resources. These organizations focused on a range of issues, including employment assistance, housing, education, and financial aid. Their aim was to ensure that soldiers and veterans could successfully reintegrate into society and lead fulfilling lives after their service.

Furthermore, the military itself recognized the importance of support systems for soldiers and veterans. They implemented programs such as the Yellow Ribbon Reintegration Program, which aimed to help service members transition back to civilian life. This program provided access to information, resources, and support networks to facilitate a smooth reintegration process.

Importantly, the psychological and emotional toll on soldiers and veterans was acknowledged, and efforts were made to address these issues. Mental health professionals were embedded within military units to provide immediate support and counseling. Additionally, peer support programs were established, allowing soldiers and veterans to connect with others who had shared similar experiences.

While these support systems were undoubtedly beneficial, there were also challenges and controversies surrounding their effectiveness and accessibility. Some soldiers and veterans faced difficulties in accessing the resources they needed, leading to a growing awareness of the gaps in the support system. Furthermore, the long-term impact of the psychological toll on soldiers and veterans remains an ongoing concern.

In conclusion, the support systems for soldiers and veterans during and after Operation Iraqi Freedom played a vital role in addressing their physical, psychological, and emotional needs. The provision of healthcare services, the establishment of non-profit organizations, and military-led programs all contributed to ensuring that soldiers and veterans had access to the support they needed. However, ongoing efforts are required to address the challenges and controversies that surround these systems, in order to provide the best possible care for those who served in this conflict.

Challenges in Reintegration and Rehabilitation

The invasion and occupation of Iraq during Operation Iraqi Freedom presented numerous challenges in terms of reintegrating and rehabilitating the country and its people. This subchapter will delve into the multifaceted issues faced in the aftermath of the conflict, specifically focusing on the post-war struggles of both the Iraqi population and the military personnel involved.

One of the primary challenges in reintegration and rehabilitation was the immense destruction and loss of infrastructure caused by the invasion. The military strategy and tactics employed during Operation Iraqi Freedom, including aerial bombings and ground assaults, resulted in widespread damage to schools, hospitals, roads, and other vital facilities. The process of rebuilding these structures and creating a stable environment for the Iraqi people posed significant logistical and financial hurdles.

Additionally, the political implications and aftermath of the U.S.-led invasion had a profound impact on the reintegration efforts. The removal of Saddam Hussein's regime left a power vacuum, leading to a period of instability and sectarian violence. This created a challenging environment for rehabilitation, as different factions vied for control and engaged in armed conflicts. The task of fostering reconciliation and establishing a functional government became an uphill battle.

Furthermore, the humanitarian efforts and civilian casualties during the invasion added another layer of complexity to the reintegration process. The invasion resulted in a significant loss of life, displacement of millions of Iraqis, and the disruption of essential services. Addressing the needs of the affected population and ensuring their well-being became vital in achieving successful reintegration and rehabilitation.

The media coverage and propaganda surrounding Operation Iraqi Freedom also played a crucial role in shaping public opinion and influencing the challenges faced during reintegration. The portrayal of the invasion as a liberation or occupation impacted how Iraqis and the international community perceived the U.S.-led forces. This perception, whether positive or negative, influenced the interactions between the military personnel and the local population, affecting the overall process of reintegration.

Moreover, the psychological and emotional toll on soldiers and veterans of Operation Iraqi Freedom presented a unique challenge. The experiences of combat, witnessing civilian casualties, and the stress of extended deployments led to various mental health issues among military personnel. Providing adequate support and rehabilitation services for these individuals became crucial in their successful reintegration into civilian life.

In conclusion, the challenges in reintegration and rehabilitation following the U.S.-led invasion of Iraq were vast and multifaceted. The destruction of infrastructure, political instability, humanitarian issues, media coverage, the psychological toll on soldiers, and many other factors complicated the process. Understanding and addressing these challenges is essential to gain a comprehensive understanding of the repercussions of Operation Iraqi Freedom and to navigate future conflicts and post-war situations effectively.

Chapter 10: Legal Aspects and Controversies Surrounding the Invasion and Occupation of Iraq

Legality of the Invasion under International Law

The invasion and subsequent occupation of Iraq by the United States and its coalition forces has been a subject of intense debate and controversy since its inception. One of the key aspects that historians and researchers have delved into is the legality of this military action under international law. Understanding the legal framework surrounding the invasion is essential in comprehending the various aspects and implications of Operation Iraqi Freedom.

The invasion of Iraq in 2003, carried out under the premise of eliminating Saddam Hussein's regime and alleged possession of weapons of mass destruction, raised significant questions regarding its compliance with international law. The primary legal justification cited by the United States was the right to self-defense under Article 51 of the United Nations Charter. However, this argument was widely contested as Iraq was not perceived as an imminent threat to the United States or its allies.

Another legal aspect that sparked controversy was the absence of a United Nations Security Council (UNSC) resolution specifically authorizing the invasion. The United States claimed that previous UNSC resolutions, such as Resolution 687, provided sufficient legal basis for military intervention. Nevertheless, many historians and legal experts argue that only a new and explicit resolution could have legitimized the invasion under international law.

Furthermore, the question of whether the invasion complied with the doctrine of humanitarian intervention was also raised. Advocates of this doctrine argue that military action can be justified on humanitarian grounds, such as preventing or ending widespread human rights abuses. However, critics contend that the humanitarian situation in Iraq did not meet the threshold required for such intervention.

The legality of the invasion also intersects with the issue of the hunt for weapons of mass destruction (WMDs). The alleged presence of WMDs in Iraq was a pivotal factor used to justify the invasion. However, post-invasion investigations failed to find concrete evidence supporting these claims, leading to further doubts about the legality of the action taken.

In conclusion, the legality of the invasion and occupation of Iraq under international law remains a matter of contention and debate. Historians studying Operation Iraqi Freedom must critically analyze the legal justifications put forth by the United States and the international community. By examining the various legal aspects and controversies surrounding the invasion, researchers can gain a comprehensive understanding of the intricate legal framework that underpinned this significant event in modern history.

Use of Force and the Doctrine of Preemptive Self-Defense

The use of force has been a highly contentious issue in the context of the invasion and occupation of Iraq. This subchapter explores the legal aspects and controversies surrounding the doctrine of preemptive self-defense, which played a significant role in justifying the U.S.-led invasion of Iraq during Operation Iraqi Freedom.

The doctrine of preemptive self-defense posits that a state is justified in using force to prevent an imminent attack from another state. It is based on the assumption that waiting for an attack to occur would be too late to effectively defend oneself. Proponents argue that preemptive action is necessary to protect national security and prevent potential harm to its citizens.

In the case of Iraq, the U.S. government invoked this doctrine to justify its decision to invade the country. The argument put forth was that Saddam Hussein's regime possessed weapons of mass destruction (WMDs) and posed an imminent threat to the United States and its allies. The evidence presented, however, turned out to be flawed, leading to significant controversy and criticism.

Critics argue that the doctrine of preemptive self-defense was misapplied in the case of Iraq. They contend that the intelligence used to justify the invasion was either manipulated or faulty, and that there was no imminent threat from Iraq. This has raised questions about the legality and legitimacy of the invasion, as well as the credibility of intelligence agencies involved.

The controversy surrounding the use of force and the doctrine of preemptive self-defense in Iraq has had far-reaching implications. It has called into question the credibility of the U.S. government, damaged international relations, and fueled anti-war sentiment both domestically and worldwide. Additionally, the invasion and subsequent occupation of Iraq have had significant political, economic, and humanitarian ramifications.

Historians studying Operation Iraqi Freedom, military strategy and tactics, political implications, and the aftermath of the U.S.-led invasion will find this subchapter crucial in understanding the legal aspects and controversies surrounding the invasion and occupation of Iraq. It sheds light on the justifications used to employ force, the role of intelligence, and the subsequent impact on international relations, public opinion, and protests against Operation Iraqi Freedom.

By critically examining the use of force and the doctrine of preemptive self-defense, this subchapter contributes to a comprehensive understanding of the complex and multifaceted nature of the Iraq war, providing historians with valuable insights into one of the most controversial military campaigns of the 21st century.

Treatment of Prisoners and Violations of Human Rights

The treatment of prisoners and the violations of human rights during the invasion and occupation of Iraq have been subject to intense scrutiny and controversy. This subchapter aims to shed light on the various aspects surrounding this issue, highlighting the legal implications and debates that have emerged.

One of the most significant concerns regarding the treatment of prisoners was the widespread reports of torture and abuse in detention facilities, most notably at Abu Ghraib prison. The revelations of the infamous photographs depicting the mistreatment of detainees shocked the world and triggered international condemnation. Historians analyzing the events surrounding the invasion and occupation of Iraq cannot overlook the impact of these violations on the overall perception of the operation and the subsequent political fallout.

This subchapter delves into the legal aspects surrounding the treatment of prisoners, examining the applicability of international human rights laws and the Geneva Conventions. The debate over the classification of detainees as either prisoners of war or unlawful combatants further complicates the issue, as it determines the level of protection they are entitled to under international law.

Furthermore, the subchapter explores the role of intelligence gathering and interrogations, particularly in relation to the search for weapons of mass destruction. It examines the ethical boundaries and controversies surrounding enhanced interrogation techniques employed by U.S. forces, such as waterboarding, and the impact they had on detainees' rights.

In addition, the subchapter addresses the accountability and responsibility of both U.S. military personnel and the political leadership for the violations committed. It investigates the legal mechanisms employed to hold individuals accountable for their actions and the challenges faced in achieving justice for the victims.

Lastly, the subchapter considers the impact of these violations on public opinion, both domestically and internationally, and the subsequent protests against the invasion and occupation. Understanding the public's perception and response to the treatment of prisoners is crucial for historians analyzing the broader implications of Operation Iraqi Freedom.

Overall, this subchapter aims to provide historians with a comprehensive understanding of the treatment of prisoners and violations of human rights during the invasion and occupation of Iraq. By examining the legal aspects, controversies, and consequences of these actions, it offers valuable insights into this dark chapter of history.

Accountability for War Crimes and Legal Implications

In the tumultuous aftermath of the U.S.-led invasion of Iraq and the removal of Saddam Hussein, the issue of accountability for war crimes and the legal implications of such actions have become subjects of intense debate and controversy. Historians studying the Operation Iraqi Freedom and its consequences cannot ignore the crucial role that accountability plays in understanding the complexities of this conflict.

The invasion and subsequent occupation of Iraq witnessed numerous instances of alleged war crimes committed by both the coalition forces and various factions within Iraq. These crimes, including unlawful killings, torture, and mistreatment of detainees, have raised serious questions about the adherence to international humanitarian law and the legal implications for those responsible.

One of the primary challenges in addressing accountability for war crimes in Iraq lies in determining the jurisdiction and legal framework applicable to these cases. The U.S. government's assertion of immunity for its personnel under the principle of sovereign immunity has often hindered efforts to prosecute individuals responsible for war crimes. This has led to criticism and accusations of impunity, further fueling controversies surrounding the invasion.

The establishment of the International Criminal Court (ICC) in 2002 provided a potential avenue for addressing accountability for war crimes committed during the invasion and occupation. However, the United States, along with Iraq, has not ratified the Rome Statute, thus limiting the ICC's jurisdiction over the situation. This has resulted in a fragmented approach to accountability, with some cases being prosecuted domestically and others falling outside the purview of international bodies.

Moreover, the legal implications of war crimes extend beyond individual accountability. The actions of military commanders, the responsibility of states in preventing war crimes, and the duty to provide reparations to victims are all vital aspects that historians must consider. The failure to hold individuals and states accountable not only erodes the rule of law but also perpetuates cycles of violence and impunity.

Understanding the legal aspects and controversies surrounding the invasion and occupation of Iraq is essential for historians examining Operation Iraqi Freedom. By delving into the complexities of accountability for war crimes, historians can shed light on the challenges faced in seeking justice, the implications for international law, and the lessons to be learned from this contentious chapter in history.

In conclusion, accountability for war crimes and the legal implications of such acts remain contentious issues in the context of the U.S.-led invasion of Iraq. Historians examining Operation Iraqi Freedom must carefully consider the complexities surrounding accountability, the challenges in prosecuting war crimes, and the broader implications for international law. By addressing these issues, a comprehensive understanding of the invasion and its aftermath can be achieved, contributing to a more nuanced historical narrative.

Chapter 11: Public Opinion and Protests against Operation Iraqi Freedom

Anti-War Movements and Global Protests

The invasion and occupation of Iraq during Operation Iraqi Freedom sparked a wave of global protests and anti-war movements that reverberated across continents. This subchapter delves into the legal aspects, debates, and consequences of these movements, analyzing their impact on the U.S.-led invasion of Iraq and the removal of Saddam Hussein. Addressing historians and enthusiasts of Operation Iraqi Freedom, it aims to provide a comprehensive understanding of the diverse range of voices and perspectives that emerged during this tumultuous period.

The anti-war movements and global protests against the Iraq War were a reflection of widespread public sentiment and opposition to military intervention. Protests erupted in major cities worldwide, drawing millions of people who vehemently opposed the invasion. Historians have since studied these movements to understand their origins, dynamics, and effectiveness in shaping public opinion and influencing government policies.

This subchapter begins by examining the legal aspects surrounding the invasion. It explores the arguments put forth by those who challenged the legality of the war, highlighting key international laws and treaties that were invoked to question the actions of the U.S. and its coalition partners. The chapter also delves into the legal implications of the war, including the controversial issue of regime change and the subsequent occupation of Iraq.

Furthermore, this subchapter explores the debates that emerged within the anti-war movements themselves. While the overarching goal of these movements was to prevent the war and end the occupation, they encompassed a wide array of perspectives and strategies. From pacifist organizations advocating non-violence to radical groups demanding immediate withdrawal, this subchapter analyzes the diverse approaches taken by these movements and the debates that ensued.

Finally, the chapter examines the consequences of the anti-war movements and global protests. It assesses their impact on public opinion, government decision-making processes, and the perception of the war in the international community. By analyzing the successes and limitations of these movements, historians can gain valuable insights into the role of public dissent in shaping foreign policy and military interventions.

In conclusion, the subchapter on Anti-War Movements and Global Protests offers a nuanced exploration of the legal aspects, debates, and consequences surrounding the U.S.-led invasion of Iraq and the removal of Saddam Hussein. By delving into the perspectives of historians and enthusiasts of Operation Iraqi Freedom, this chapter aims to shed light on the multifaceted nature of the anti-war movements and their lasting impact on the Iraq War narrative.

Divisions within Public Opinion

Public opinion played a significant role in shaping the events surrounding the U.S.-led invasion of Iraq and the subsequent occupation. However, it was far from being a monolithic entity. Divisions within public opinion were evident both domestically within the United States and internationally, reflecting the complex and controversial nature of the invasion.

Within the United States, the decision to invade Iraq was met with a range of opinions. On one side, there were those who strongly supported the invasion, arguing that it was necessary to remove Saddam Hussein from power and to prevent the spread of weapons of mass destruction. These supporters believed that the invasion would lead to a safer and more stable Middle East.

On the other side of the spectrum, there were those who vehemently opposed the invasion. Critics argued that the invasion was unjustified, as there was insufficient evidence to support the claims of weapons of mass destruction. They also raised concerns about the legality of the invasion and the potential for a protracted and costly occupation.

These divisions within public opinion were reflected in widespread protests and demonstrations across the United States and in other parts of the world. Anti-war activists, students, and other concerned citizens took to the streets to voice their opposition to the invasion. Their protests were often fueled by a deep skepticism of the government's motives and a belief that the invasion was driven by ulterior motives, such as control over Iraq's oil reserves.

Internationally, public opinion was similarly divided. While some countries, such as the United Kingdom, joined the United States in the invasion, others expressed strong opposition. Many European nations, as well as countries in the Middle East and elsewhere, condemned the invasion as a violation of international law and an example of American imperialism.

These divisions within public opinion had far-reaching implications for the invasion and occupation of Iraq. They influenced political decision-making, military strategy, and the perception of the United States and its coalition partners both at home and abroad. The protests and opposition to the invasion also contributed to a growing sense of disillusionment and mistrust among the American public, as well as in other parts of the world.

Understanding the divisions within public opinion is crucial for historians examining the invasion and occupation of Iraq. It provides valuable insights into the complexities and controversies surrounding the events, as well as the broader implications for international relations, military strategy, and the role of public sentiment in shaping political decisions. By examining the various perspectives and arguments within public opinion, historians can gain a more nuanced understanding of one of the most contentious episodes in recent history.

Media Influence on Public Perception

In the era of information overload, the media plays a crucial role in shaping public perception. This subchapter explores the profound impact of media on public opinion during the Operation Iraqi Freedom – the U.S.-led invasion of Iraq and the subsequent removal of Saddam Hussein. Examining the legal aspects and debates surrounding this contentious period, it becomes evident that the media's influence on public perception cannot be underestimated.

During the invasion and occupation of Iraq, the media became a powerful tool in the hands of governments, shaping narratives and molding public opinion. Historians studying this era must recognize the media's role in disseminating information, framing events, and ultimately influencing public perception. The media's portrayal of the invasion and the justifications provided for it had a significant impact on how the public perceived the actions of the United States and its allies.

One critical aspect of media influence was the coverage of the initial justifications for the invasion, primarily the alleged presence of weapons of mass destruction (WMDs) in Iraq. The media played a pivotal role in echoing the government's claims, amplifying the perceived threat posed by Iraq and Saddam Hussein. Through repetitive coverage, the media helped to solidify public support for the invasion, leading to a widespread belief in the necessity of military action.

However, as the occupation unfolded, discrepancies between the media narrative and the realities on the ground began to emerge. The media's portrayal of the war shifted from one of swift victory and liberation to one of protracted conflict and chaos. This shift in perception was influenced by the media's coverage of the insurgency, civilian casualties, and the challenges faced by coalition forces. As a result, public opinion started to waver, with increasing skepticism toward the government's motives and the effectiveness of the mission.

Moreover, the media's coverage of the war was not without controversy. Accusations of biased reporting, both pro-war and anti-war, were rampant. Some argued that the media failed to critically question the government's justifications for the invasion, while others accused it of undermining the war effort by highlighting negative aspects. These debates highlight the media's power to shape public perception and the ethical dilemmas faced by journalists in reporting on conflicts.

In conclusion, the media's influence on public perception during the Operation Iraqi Freedom was profound. Historians studying this period must recognize the media's role in shaping narratives, framing events, and ultimately influencing public opinion. The coverage of the invasion and occupation of Iraq by the media played a significant role in shaping public perception, both in justifying the initial military action and later creating doubts and skepticism. Understanding the complexities of media influence is essential to comprehending the broader legal aspects and debates surrounding this controversial chapter in history.

Legacy of Protests and Impact on Government Policy

Throughout history, protests have played a significant role in shaping government policies and bringing about social change. The legacy of protests during the U.S.-led invasion of Iraq, known as Operation Iraqi Freedom, has had a profound impact on government policy and the subsequent political landscape. This subchapter examines the enduring effects of these protests and their implications for the invasion and occupation of Iraq.

The protests against Operation Iraqi Freedom were a global phenomenon, with millions of people taking to the streets in cities across the world. Historians studying this period recognize these protests as one of the largest global demonstrations in history. The opposition to the invasion was multifaceted, encompassing concerns about the legality, morality, and potential consequences of the military intervention.

The protests had a profound impact on government policy, both domestically and internationally. In many countries, public opinion against the invasion forced governments to reconsider their support for the war effort. For example, in the United Kingdom, the large-scale protests contributed to a significant decline in public support for the government's decision to join the coalition forces. This, in turn, put pressure on political leaders to justify their actions and caused divisions within ruling parties.

Internationally, the protests also influenced the stance of other governments towards the invasion. Countries that were initially supportive of the U.S.-led coalition, such as Germany and France, faced internal pressure to distance themselves from the war due to the opposition voiced by their citizens. This led to strained relationships within the international community and influenced subsequent decisions regarding the occupation and reconstruction efforts in Iraq.

Furthermore, the legacy of these protests can be seen in the increased scrutiny and debate surrounding government policies and military interventions. The public outcry against Operation Iraqi Freedom prompted a reevaluation of the decision-making processes that led to the invasion. Governments were compelled to be more transparent and accountable to their citizens, with demands for greater justifications for military actions and clearer exit strategies.

In conclusion, the legacy of protests against Operation Iraqi Freedom has had a lasting impact on government policy. The massive demonstrations and widespread opposition to the invasion forced governments to reassess their positions and led to increased public scrutiny of military interventions. Historians studying this period recognize the significance of these protests in shaping the political landscape both nationally and internationally. The impact of these protests highlights the power of public opinion and the role of civil society in influencing government decisions.

Conclusion: Lessons Learned and Historical Analysis of Operation Iraqi Freedom

The U.S.-led invasion of Iraq and the subsequent occupation of the country, known as Operation Iraqi Freedom, has been one of the most controversial military campaigns in recent history. As historians, it is our duty to critically analyze this operation, considering its legal aspects, military strategy and tactics, political implications, humanitarian efforts, media coverage, international relations, intelligence, economic impact, psychological toll on soldiers, and public opinion. By examining these various aspects, we can draw important lessons from this historical event and gain a deeper understanding of its consequences.

First and foremost, Operation Iraqi Freedom highlighted the importance of thorough legal justifications for military interventions. The controversial nature of the invasion raised questions about the legitimacy of the war under international law, particularly in the absence of clear evidence of weapons of mass destruction in Iraq. This legal ambiguity has led to ongoing debates and discussions among legal scholars and policymakers, urging us to carefully consider the criteria for future military interventions.

From a military standpoint, the invasion demonstrated the significance of comprehensive planning and coordination of military strategy and tactics. The swift and successful capture of Baghdad was followed by a prolonged insurgency, emphasizing the importance of not only winning the initial battle but also effectively managing the post-conflict situation. The lessons learned from Operation Iraqi Freedom have influenced subsequent military campaigns and counterinsurgency efforts.

Furthermore, the political implications and aftermath of the U.S.-led invasion of Iraq cannot be ignored. The removal of Saddam Hussein resulted in a power vacuum that led to sectarian violence and political instability. This underscores the need for a well-thought-out plan for post-conflict governance and the importance of understanding the complexities of the region before undertaking military interventions.

Operation Iraqi Freedom also shed light on the humanitarian efforts and civilian casualties during the invasion. The impact on the civilian population and the challenges in providing aid and assistance highlighted the need for careful consideration of the potential consequences and the responsibility to protect vulnerable populations in future conflicts.

The media coverage and propaganda surrounding Operation Iraqi Freedom played a significant role in shaping public opinion and influencing international relations. The dissemination of information, both accurate and misleading, had a profound impact on the perception of the war, underscoring the importance of media literacy and critical analysis of news sources.

Additionally, the hunt for weapons of mass destruction highlighted the role of intelligence in shaping military decisions. The failure to find substantial evidence of these weapons raised questions about the intelligence gathering process and the need for reliable and accurate information before engaging in military action.

Economically, the invasion and subsequent reconstruction efforts had a substantial impact on Iraq's economy, as well as the global economy. The cost of the war, coupled with the challenges of rebuilding infrastructure and stabilizing the country, raised concerns about the long-term economic consequences of military interventions.

Operation Iraqi Freedom also took a psychological and emotional toll on the soldiers and veterans involved. The experiences of combat and the challenges of reintegrating into civilian life underscore the need for comprehensive support systems and mental health services for those who serve in future conflicts.

From a legal perspective, the invasion and occupation of Iraq raised numerous controversies, including questions of sovereignty, international law, and the legitimacy of military action. The legal aspects of this operation continue to be debated and analyzed, shaping our understanding of the limitations and responsibilities of states in international affairs.

Lastly, public opinion and protests against Operation Iraqi Freedom highlighted the importance of democratic accountability and the power of collective action. The opposition to the war sparked a global movement and demonstrated the role of public opinion in shaping political decisions.

In conclusion, the lessons learned from Operation Iraqi Freedom are multifaceted and have far-reaching implications. As historians, it is our duty to critically analyze this complex event, considering its legal, military, political, humanitarian, media, international, intelligence, economic, psychological, and public opinion aspects. By doing so, we can contribute to a deeper understanding of this controversial invasion and occupation, allowing us to learn from the past and make more informed decisions in the future.